The Brilliant CALCULATOR

HOW MATHEMATICIAN

Edith Clarke

HELPED ELECTRIFY AMERICA

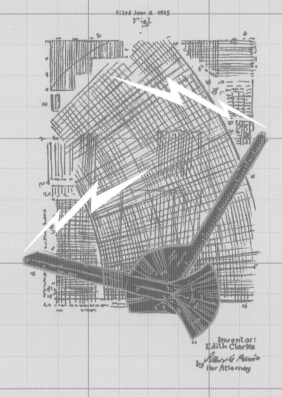

(ILLUSTRATED BY)

√‾JAN LOWER + SUSAN REAGAN

CALKINS CREEK

AN IMPRINT OF ASTRA BOOKS FOR YOUNG READERS

New York

MATH plus GIRLS
EQUALS
ELECTRICAL ENGINEERS

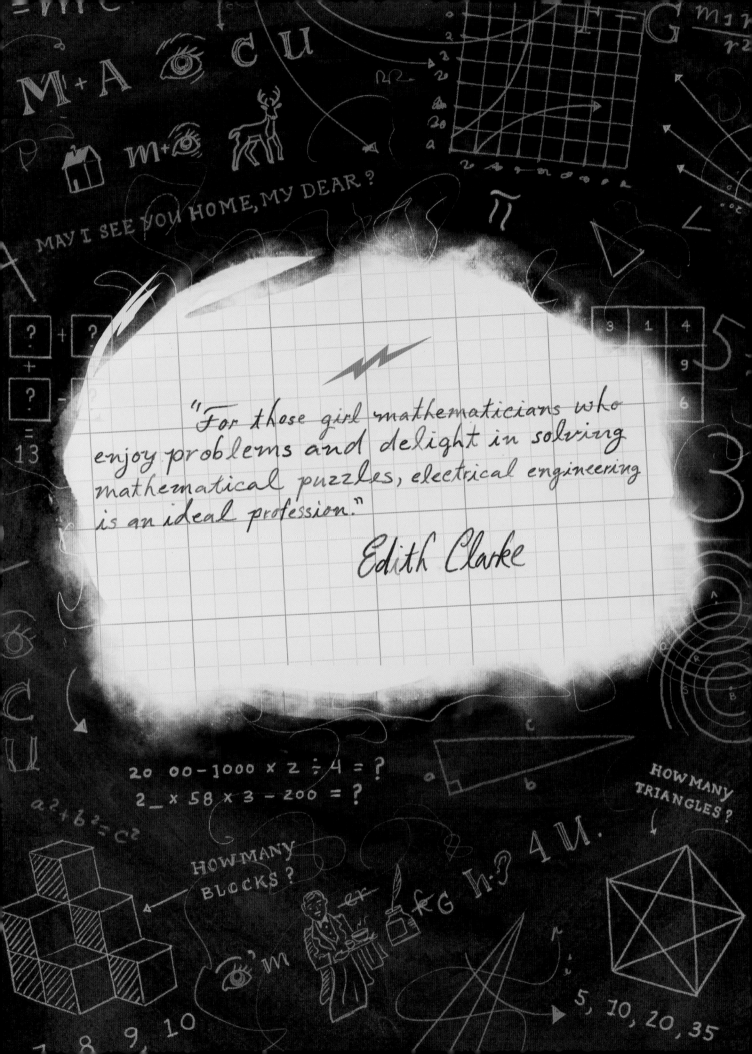

"For those girl mathematicians who enjoy problems and delight in solving mathematical puzzles, electrical engineering is an ideal profession."

Edith Clarke

Edith Clarke devoured numbers. Conquered calculations. Cracked puzzles. Breezed through brainteasers. And triumphed in the math contests at her country school.

$$12 + 4 \div 2 = 14$$
$$8 - 4 + 2 = 6$$
$$44 + 22 \times 3 - 40 = 70$$
$$12 \div 6$$
$$80 \div 4 \times 5 - 50 = 50$$
$$15 - 9 \times 20 + 100 = -65$$
$$\times 30 \div 4 \times 2 - .5 = 749.5$$
$$\times 3 \times 5 - 225 \div 3 = 1,425$$
$$2000 - 100 \times 2 \div 4 - 1,950$$
$$2 \times 58 \times 3 - \qquad 48$$
$$100 \qquad$$

One of seven girls and two boys on her Maryland farm, Edith dreamed of building railroads, dams, and bridges. And traveling the world.

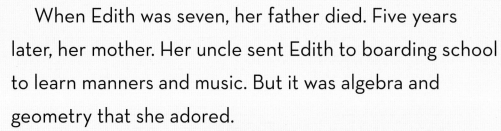

When Edith was seven, her father died. Five years later, her mother. Her uncle sent Edith to boarding school to learn manners and music. But it was algebra and geometry that she adored.

Edith finished school as the twentieth century began. Skyscrapers towered over sidewalks. Rickety automobiles putt-putted along. Inventors tested flying machines. Edith saw that modern times needed the numbers she loved. Measurements and computations made dreams become reality. Edith longed to use math to help build America.

Too ambitious, the grown-ups scolded. Girls belong on the farm.

But when she received money her parents had left her, she defied her family—and spent the money on college. To prepare, she read history and literature, hired a tutor to learn Latin, and taught herself ancient Greek.

Audentes fortuna juvat.

Disce verum laborem.

Nosce te ipsum.

"When I was a child, I thought I would like to be a civil engineer. I lacked the courage, however, because in those days women just did not do anything so bold."

Edith Clarke

NO GIRL ENGINEERS

Edith entered Vassar College at the age most students graduate. She rose to the top of her class—though her Greek accent was hilarious—and left in 1908 with a degree in mathematics and astronomy.

Edith knew few careers welcomed women, so she taught: physics at a girls' school, then math at a college . . . until she became perilously ill. Edith feared she would die, like her parents—and four of her siblings—but she survived.

$E = mc^2$

$a = \dfrac{\Delta v}{\Delta t}$

$v = v_0 + at$

$w = w_0 + \alpha t$

$\Phi_B = \int_S \vec{B} \cdot d\vec{A}$

$Q = mc \, \Delta T$

$Q = Lm$

Edith found work as a human "computor" with engineers building the first phone wires across America. She computed thousands of equations, explained her mathematical solutions, and helped invent a slide rule to speed calculations. When she learned that voices as electric signals faded over many miles of wire, Edith needed to understand *why*.

At night in engineering classes she investigated ELECTRICITY. It was impossible to hold. It was dangerous and deadly. It zoomed thousands of miles in only a second!

Edith discovered ELECTRIC POWER WIRES
weakened and broke. If they were overloaded, they
could burst into flames. Transporting electric power was
her kind of riddle—one that Edith was determined to solve.
She left the computors at the telephone company for the
Massachusetts Institute of Technology.

Edith graduated in just a year and a half—but no one wanted a *woman* engineer. Once more she directed computors, for a company building power lines. And, in her free time, Edith tackled the tangled problem of transmission line design—on her own!

$R' = R\frac{50}{f}$, and a new length of line

l = Length of line in miles

$E_g / \sqrt{3} =$ VOLTS

Her mind's eye saw numbers arranged on a graph.
Electric flow. Length of line in miles. Generator force
pushing power into wires. All part of a transmission
line's plan.

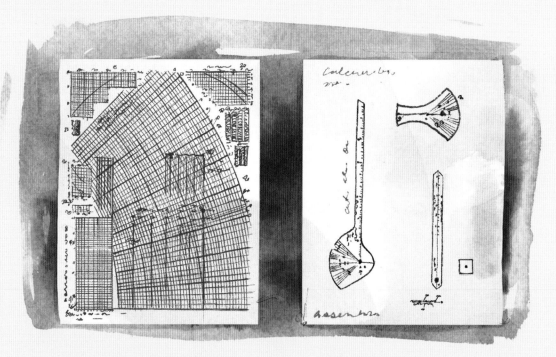

Edith filled a sheet of paper with lines, arcs, and grids.
On another she drew wings—one long and two short—
etched with lines and numbers.

Edith concentrated. She calculated. She paused—and began again.

Edith adjusted numbers and reconstructed. At last she glued the pieces on cardboard, cut them all out with scissors, and pinned the wings to the bottom of the graph.

$$-j16\pi^3 f^3 L C^2 R\}$$

$$ZY = 1z.1y = 1^2(R+j2\pi f^2 L)(j2\pi f \dot{C})$$
$$= 1z\{-4\pi^2 f^2 LC + j2\pi f CR\}$$

$z^2 y^2$ may be obtained as vectors

substitution of these values in $\cosh\sqrt{ZY}$ and in the infinite series gives

$$1 + \frac{ZY}{\underline{3}} + \frac{Z^2 Y^2}{\underline{4}} + \cdots = \{1 - 2\pi^2 f^2 1^2 LC + \frac{2}{3}\pi^4 f^4 1^4 L^2 C^2 -$$

and $\frac{1}{6}\pi^2 f^2 1^4 R^2 C^2 + \cdots\} + jR\{\pi f 1^2 C - \frac{2}{3}\pi^3 f^3 1^4 L C^2 + \cdots\}$

$$1 + \frac{ZY}{6} + \frac{Z^2 Y^2}{120} + \cdots = \{1 - \frac{2}{3}\pi^2 f^2 1^2 L C + \frac{2}{15}\pi^4 f^4 1^4 L^2 C^2 - \frac{1}{30}$$

$\pi^2 f^2 1^4 C^2 R^2 + \cdots\} + jR\{\frac{1}{3}\pi f 1^2 - \frac{2}{15}\pi^3 f^3 1^4 L C^2 + \cdots\}$ whence

$$\frac{e_g}{e_r} = \cosh\sqrt{ZY} + \frac{i_r}{e_r}Z\left(1 + \frac{ZY}{\underline{3}} + \frac{Z^2 Y^2}{\underline{5}} + \cdots\right)$$

and $\frac{i_g}{i_r} = \cosh\sqrt{ZY} + \frac{e_r}{i_r}Y\left(1 + \frac{ZY}{\underline{3}} + \frac{Z^2 Y^2}{\underline{5}} + \cdots\right)$

$\cosh z$

$$i_x Z\left(1 + \frac{ZY}{\underline{3}} + \frac{Z}{\underline{5}} \cdots\right) \qquad e x^2 = \frac{E r^2}{3},$$

and $i_g = i_r\left(1 + \frac{ZY}{\underline{3}} + \frac{Z^2 Y^2}{\underline{4}} + \cdots\right)$

$e_r Y\left(1 + \frac{ZY}{\underline{3}} + \frac{Z}{\underline{5}} \cdots\right)$

$\frac{i_r}{e_r} = \frac{\text{watts r}}{e r^2 \times 3 \times P.F_r} \times$

$\left[P.F_r b + j\left(1 - \sqrt{1 - P.F_r^2}\right)\right]$

Watts

$$\frac{e_g}{e_r} = \cosh\sqrt{ZY} + \frac{i_r}{e_r}Z\left(1 + \frac{ZY}{\underline{3}} + \cdots\right)$$

substitution expression has alt

and

$\frac{i_r}{e_r} = 10^{-3}\dfrac{K.W.r}{K.V.r^2 \times P.F.r}\times$

$\left[P.F_r + j\left(\pm\sqrt{1 - P.F.r^2}\right)\right]$

$\left[P.F.r + j\left(\pm\sqrt{1 - P.F.r^2}\right)\right]\times\phi\times\beta$

As Edith slid the wings over the grid, lines connected and moved on, meeting number after number. She solved an equation by hand, then with her paper tool. The answers matched! Again and again, using pen and paper, then graph and wings, Edith's invention was always correct!

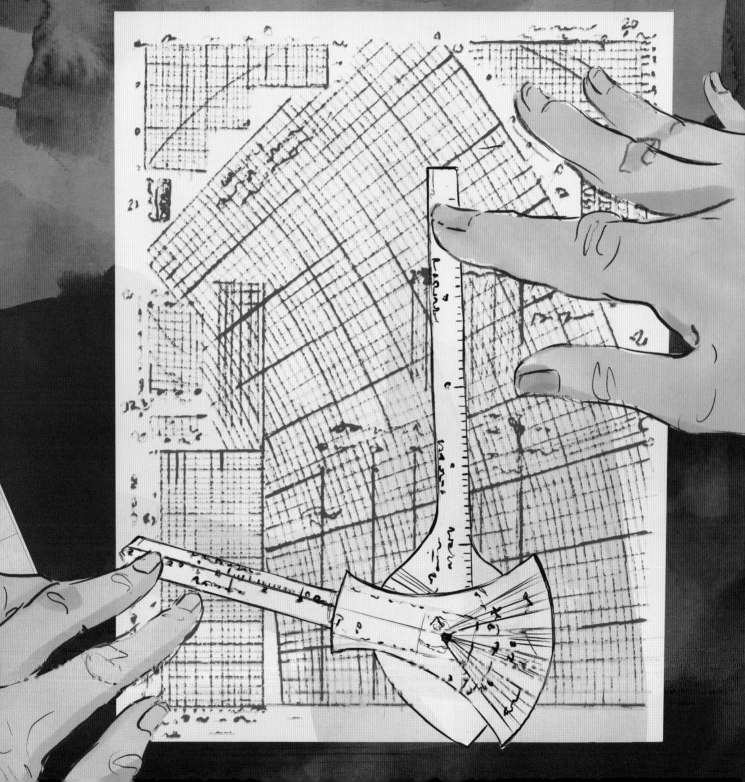

One by one the transmission engineers surveyed Edith's calculator. They solved equations—first by hand, then with her paper tool. Over and over. No errors! And her calculator was *ten times faster* than any human! In a flash, they adopted Edith's brilliant apparatus, and . . .

. . . hired Edith—America's first female electrical engineer!

"There is a future for women in engineering, and some day the only limitation will be their own lack of ability, as we are fast approaching an age in which men and women will be measured by their worth as individuals."

Edith Clarke

$\sqrt{MATH}$ + 's =

$E \varepsilon Z \varsigma H \eta$

$\Phi \varphi X \chi \Psi \psi$

20.00 - 1000 x
2 - x 58 x 3 - 200 -

$\emptyset$

Electric

NASA

AUTHOR'S NOTE

Edith Clarke at her desk in the General Electric Laboratory in Schenectady, New York

Edith Clarke insisted on receiving recognition for her remarkable Clarke Calculator and filed for a patent from the United States government soon after she invented it. She received her patent four years later—the first of three patents she was awarded in her lifetime. But she also wanted every electrical engineer in the country to be able to use her calculator right away. Before her patent was approved, she published a pattern and instructions on how to make her calculator so engineers everywhere could use it to speed up the electrification of America.

Edith claimed that her remarkable accomplishments were due only to her interests and curiosity, not to any hard work on her part. Edith's determined mind never seemed to stop: she researched, wrote, and taught her entire life. Even when she relaxed, she used her brain. She loved complicated card games and every kind of riddle, brainteaser, and mental puzzle. Edith succeeded at her dream of seeing the world; she was a passionate traveler and always kept a world atlas on her office desk to plan her adventures. Edith took a leave of absence from the General Electric Company (GE) to teach for a year in Turkey and travel in Europe, and later left her job for three months to journey beyond the Arctic Circle. When she retired, she taught electrical engineering for ten years at the University of Texas, enjoying everything about the Lone Star State. Edith loved the outdoors. She excelled at tennis, skiing, skating, and swimming, and for many years had a cottage on Lake George in upstate New York. But Edith never lost her wholehearted connection to the farmland of Maryland.

MORE ABOUT EDITH CLARKE'S CONTRIBUTIONS TO ENGINEERING

Edith's far-reaching mathematics background was unusual for an electrical engineer in the early twentieth century. She transformed complicated math theories into simple charts and graphs that any engineer could use to understand the behavior of power lines under different electric flow and weather conditions. A mathematical method Edith developed and its result are named for her: the "Clarke Transformation" and "Clarke Coordinates."

Her research on transmission set the stage for today's "Smart Electric Grid." In 1931, engineers at the Massachusetts Institute of Technology completed the development of a mechanical computer called a "Differential Analyzer" to perform complicated mathematical calculations. Weighing eighteen tons, it was a table-like arrangement of metal rods and gears driven by small electric motors. Edith Clarke was one of the few engineers permitted to use MIT's Differential Analyzer. A similar analyzer at the University of Pennsylvania was an inspiration for the first modern computer, ENIAC.

Most electric transmission networks are now "Smart Grids" with special equipment that senses electricity in the wires at different times and locations, along with real-time weather conditions.

Computers collect this information, helping to predict the need for power flow throughout the network. Because of her research using the Differential Analyzer to understand how power lines operate under different conditions, Edith is recognized as taking the first steps toward imagining the Smart Grid—almost a century ago.

In 2003, Edith Clarke was inducted into the Maryland Women's Hall of Fame. In recognition of her Clarke Calculator, Edith was inducted into the National Inventors Hall of Fame in 2015. The University of Texas created the "Edith Clarke Woman of Excellence Award" in her honor in 2016.

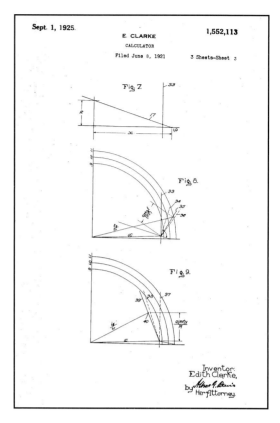

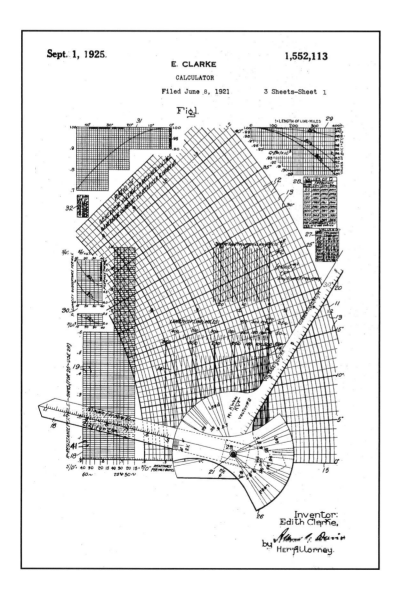

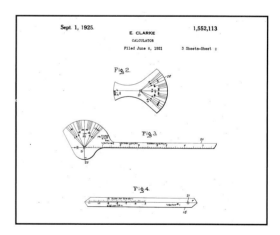

Diagrams from Edith Clarke's patent for her Clarke Calculator, granted by the U.S. Patent and Trademark Office on September 1, 1925

EDITH CLARKE AND THE AGE OF ELECTRIFICATION: A TIMELINE

In the United States, the process of bringing electric power to homes and industries began in the 1880s and continued for more than sixty years.

1882:   In New York City, electricity is sent over wires connecting generators to streetlights and buildings located up to a mile away. Companies in other cities soon begin to deliver electricity to nearby lighting customers.

1883:   On February 10, Edith Clarke is born on her family's farm in Howard County, Maryland.

Edith Clarke (left), about eight years old, with her sister Rachel, in the early 1890s

1893:   The Chicago World's Fair features a Great Hall of Electricity where families can examine electric lamps, sewing machines, fans, laundry machines, dishwashers, ovens, and other electric appliances. At night, the Fair is brilliantly lit by over 90,000 lightbulbs.

1907:   Because electric power cannot be delivered through wires over long distances, fewer than one out of every ten Americans has electricity at home.

1912:   Edith becomes a computor for a research engineer at the American Telephone and Telegraph Company in New York City. At night, she studies radio technology at Hunter College and electrical engineering at Columbia University.

1914:   World War I begins in Europe. In America, about one-third of factories rely on electricity generated nearby to run their lights and equipment.

1917:   The United States joins World War I. Factories need electric power to make military equipment. Small networks of wires are connected, but problems often occur.

1918:   World War I ends. Edith enters the Massachusetts Institute of Technology (MIT) and, in her research, applies mathematical theories to understanding the behavior of electric systems.

1919:   Edith is the first woman to graduate from MIT as an electrical engineer, with a master of science degree. She becomes director of women computors for GE's Turbine Engineering Department.

1920:   Home appliances such as electric irons, vacuum cleaners, and radios are available, but only one-third of US homes have electricity. Just over half of US factories purchase electricity from small electric companies.

1921:   Edith invents the Clarke Calculator, for which a patent is issued on September 1, 1925.

1922:   Edith is hired by GE as the first female electrical engineer in the United States.

1923: Edith publishes a paper describing how to make her Clarke Calculator so all transmission engineers can use it to work more quickly.

1926: Edith is the first woman to speak to a conference of the American Institute of Electrical Engineers, describing how mathematical theories can simplify the study of power systems.

1927: Edith receives a second patent for her invention of a method to control how much electricity can be pushed into a power line so it can be used safely at its maximum limit.

1929: More than two-thirds of manufacturing in the United States depends on electricity.

1930: The number of homes in the United States with electricity and electric appliances—two out of three—has doubled since 1920. Edith takes charge of a group of engineers at GE to study power system reliability. They solve transmission problems sent to them by companies across the country. The world's largest network of generators and high-voltage electric power lines, a ring of wires 210 miles around, begins to carry electricity in Pennsylvania and New Jersey.

1930s: Edith continues to apply mathematical theories to electrical engineering research, eventually publishing eighteen papers that she wrote or co-authored.

1931: Edith works with an early computer, the Differential Analyzer (built at MIT), which can mathematically model transmission system problems.

1935: Nine out of ten homes in or near cities and towns have power service. Only one out of ten homes and farms in the countryside has electricity.

1936: A new federal government loan program created by the Rural Electrification Act of 1936 encourages the building of electric distribution systems in rural areas.

1937: GE builds a computer-like machine called a Network Analyzer to analyze transmission systems. Edith uses it in her research.

1939: One in four farms has electric power.

1940: Edith is one of three women belonging to the American Institute of Electrical Engineers, which has a membership of 17,000.

1941: With another engineer, Edith publishes the first mathematical research on transmission lines over 300 miles long.

1943: Based on lectures she gave to other engineers at GE during the 1920s and 1930s, Edith publishes a book on power systems for both working engineers and students that becomes an essential text for many years.

1944: A patent is issued for Edith Clarke's third invention, an electrical circuit.

1945: Edith Clarke retires from GE to her farm in Maryland.

1947: Edith becomes America's first female electrical engineering professor, at the University of Texas. She publishes the second volume of her engineering textbook in 1950. Popular with students, she teaches for ten years and returns each summer to her farm.

1953: Nine out of ten rural homes and farms have electric service.

1957: Edith retires again.

1959: Edith Clarke dies on October 29.

Human "computors" calculate bonuses owed to veterans in one of the computing divisions at the United States Department of the Treasury.

GLOSSARY

circuit: An arrangement of wires designed to move electricity from one place to another, such as from a generator to a user.

civil engineer: An engineer who designs, constructs, and maintains buildings, roads, bridges, canals, airports, railways, dams, and other structures that people use every day.

current: The rate of flow of an electric charge (electrons) in a circuit.

ENIAC: The Electronic Numerical Integrator and Computer (ENIAC), the first electronic general-purpose digital computer, began operation in 1946. It could be programmed to solve many types of problems. One hour of ENIAC computing time replaced 2,400 hours of human calculating work.

generator: A power source, meaning a device that converts mechanical energy (created by the force of steam, water, or wind in a machine called a turbine) to electric power that can flow over a circuit (usually a network of electric wires) to an electricity user.

resistance: The measure of opposition to the flow of electric current. Some materials, like rubber, have a higher resistance, while others, like metal, have a lower resistance.

slide rule: A wooden or plastic ruler-like tool with a sliding strip in the center. Both the ruler and the strip are marked with numbers and lines. Slide rules are used for rapid, complex calculations.

transmission: The movement of large quantities of electric energy from a generating source, such as a power plant, over high-voltage lines, to an electric substation or substations where it is converted to lower voltages for delivery to customers.

voltage: The pressure from a power source that pushes electrons (current) through the electric circuit, enabling them to do work such as lighting a bulb or running a machine.

A FEW MORE WOMEN MATHEMATICIANS, ENGINEERS, AND INVENTORS

Margaret Eloise Knight (1838–1914) invented a machine that folded and glued paper into flat-bottomed bags like those we use today. She was awarded over a dozen patents for her inventions: the bag machine, a window frame, a numbering machine, improvements to rotary engines, and many tools. At age twelve, working in a cotton mill, she invented a safety device to protect workers from flying metal that erupted from broken mechanical looms.

Harriet Williams Russell Strong (1844–1926) learned about water from drilling wells to grow orange and walnut trees. She received her first patent in 1887 for a design for a river dam and water reservoir plan, and another patent in 1894 for a new method to store large amounts of water. She received medals for these inventions at the 1893 Chicago World's Fair. Her ideas aided in the design of large dams and reservoirs in the western United States in the 1930s.

Katharine Burr Blodgett (1898–1979) covered glass with extremely thin layers of oil that prevented the glass from reflecting light while still remaining see-through. Non-reflective glass was used in movie cameras, submarine periscopes, and military spy cameras. She was awarded six patents for her inventions, which included methods for melting ice from aircraft wings.

Mária Telkes (1900–1995), known as the "Sun Queen," invented a device that uses solar power to make clean, drinkable water from sea water. She also invented a solar powered oven and helped the United States government develop the first completely solar-powered home. She received more than twenty patents for her inventions.

Katherine Johnson (1918–2020) was a mathematician who, with other women mathematicians, worked as a human computor for America's space program. She calculated the flight paths of the first American in space and the first American orbit around the Earth. She helped to calculate the path for the first Moon landing. She later worked on the Space Shuttle program and the plans for the Mars Mission.

Yvonne Brill (1924–2013), a mathematician and chemist, invented a more reliable and efficient rocket engine that was designed to save fuel and allow more equipment to be carried into space. She received a patent for the design, which is now used throughout the space industry. She contributed to the rocket designs for the first weather satellite, for American missions to the Moon, and for a space mission to observe the planet Mars.

Erna Schneider Hoover (1926–) is a mathematician who revolutionized telecommunications by inventing a computerized method for connecting telephone calls during very busy calling times, preventing telephone networks from becoming overloaded. The patent she received in 1971 for her invention was one of the first patents awarded for computer software.

Patricia E. Bath (1942–2019) was an eye doctor committed to preventing and curing blindness. She received several patents for her invention of a surgical device, the Laserphaco Probe, as well as for other laser treatment techniques. Dr. Bath was the first African American woman physician awarded a medical patent, in 1998.

SELECTED BIBLIOGRAPHY

All quotations used in the book can be found in the following sources marked with an asterisk (*).

PRIMARY SOURCES

*Alisky, Marvin. "Miss Clarke Leaves Life of 'Gentleman' Farmer to Teach UT Alecs." *Austin American-Statesman*, Feb. 11, 1947: 7. Courtesy Vassar College, Aug. 22, 2018.

Clarke, Edith. Calculator. US Patent 1,552,113, filed June 8, 1921, and issued September 1, 1925. patentimages.storage.googleapis.com/ad/d9/9b/8f8a776516f5af/US1552113.pdf.

———. *Circuit Analysis of A-C Power Systems, Vol. 1, Symmetrical and Related Components.* New York: J. Wiley & Sons, Inc., 1943.

———. "Steady-State Stability in Transmission Systems: Calculation By Means of Equivalent Circuits or Circle Diagrams." *Journal of the A.I.E.E.* 45, no. 4 (April 1926): 365.

———. "A Transmission Line Calculator." *General Electric Review* XXVI, no. 6 (June 1923): 380.

*———. "Women in Electrical Engineering." *Vassar Alumnae Magazine*, Seventy-Fifth Anniversary Addresses, Supp. II, June 1940, 11. Courtesy Vassar College. Aug. 22, 2018.

Early, Dudley. "Miss Edith Clark [*sic*]: Fate Placed Her on the Path to Fame." *Austin American-Statesman*, Oct. 10, 1948: 1.

Handy, Adelaide. "Calculates Power Transmission for General Electric Company; Miss Edith Clarke Stands on a Plane With Men In Field of Electrical Engineering." *New York Times*, Oct. 27, 1940: 52.

Overholser, Ed. "Woman Electrical Engineer Decided Against Retiring." *Wichita Falls Times*, Apr. 5, 1956: 13A.

No byline. "EE Professor Edith Clarke Likes Job." *Daily Texan*, March 16, 1947: 7.

*No byline. "Lady Engineer Celebrates Eighth Year at University." *Daily Texan*. Feb. 4, 1955: 8.

No byline. "Miss Edith Clarke, Engineer, Retires From UT Faculty After Ten Years." *Daily Texan*. Oct. 9, 1957: 5.

No byline. "Woman Addresses Electrical Institute: Miss Edith Clarke the Only One of Her Sex to Read a Paper at Engineers' Meeting." *New York Times*, Feb. 9, 1926: 14.

No byline. "Woman Mathematical Expert Wrote a Book on Electricity." *Evening Tribune* [Des Moines, IA], Jan. 20, 1944: 13.

OTHER SOURCES

Brittain, James E. "From Computor to Electrical Engineer: The Remarkable Career of Edith Clarke." *IEEE Transactions on Education*, E-28: no. 4 (Nov. 1985): 186

Goff, Alice C. *Women Can Be Engineers.* Youngstown, OH: Edwards Bros., Inc., Ann Arbor, MI, 1946.

Grier, David Alan. *When Computers Were Human.* Princeton, NJ, and Oxford, UK: Princeton University Press, 2005.

Hobbs, Amy. "Edith Clarke (1883–1959)." *Archives of Maryland, Biographical Series.* msa.maryland.gov/megafile/msa/speccol/sc3500/sc3520/014000/014065/html/14065bio.html.

Hughes, Thomas Parke. *Networks of Power: Electrification in Western Society, 1880–1930.* Baltimore: Johns Hopkins University Press, 1983.

Kass-Simon, Gabrielle, Patricia Farnes, MD, and Deborah Nash, eds. *Women of Science: Righting the Record.* Bloomington: Indiana University Press, 1990.

Layne, Margaret E., PE, ed. *Women in Engineering: Pioneers and Trailblazers.* Reston, VA: American Society of Civil Engineers Press, 2009.

Lott, Melissa. "The Engineer Who Foreshadowed the Smart Grid—in 1921." *Scientific American*, March 30, 2016. blogs.scientificamerican.com/plugged-in/the-engineer-who-foreshadowed-the-smart-grid-in-1921.

Maryland Commission for Women. "Maryland Women's Hall of Fame: Edith Clarke, 2003." msa.maryland.gov/msa/educ/exhibits/womenshallfame/html/clarke.html.

FURTHER READING
Bardoe, Cheryl. *Nothing Stopped Sophie: The Story of Unshakable Mathematician Sophie Germain*, illustrated by Barbara McClintock. New York: Little, Brown and Company, 2018.

Ignotofsky, Rachel. *Women in Science: 50 Fearless Pioneers Who Changed the World.* Berkeley: Ten Speed Press, 2016.

Marsico, Katie. *Electricity Investigations.* Minneapolis: Lerner Publications, 2018.

Parker, Steve. *DK Eyewitness Books: Electricity.* New York: Penguin Random House, 2013.

Rusch, Elizabeth. *Electrical Wizard: How Nikola Tesla Lit Up the World*, illustrated by Oliver Dominguez. Candlewick Biographies. Somerville, MA: Candlewick Press, 2013.

Shetterly, Margot Lee. *Hidden Figures: The True Story of Four Black Women and the Space Race*, illustrated by Laura Freeman. New York: HarperCollins, 2018.

Websites active at time of publication

ACKNOWLEDGMENTS

Many thanks to Vassar College for documents on Edith's education and career, and to Martha Anne Clark for Edith's nominating materials for the Maryland Women's Hall of Fame. Special thanks to Payman Dehghanian, assistant professor of electrical engineering at George Washington University, John G. Kassakian, professor of electrical engineering, emeritus, at the Massachusetts Institute of Technology, Constantine Caramanis, professor of computer and electrical engineering at the University of Texas (Austin), and to mathematician Alison F. Greene, for providing helpful technical clarifications to the manuscript. Very special thanks to the late Hugh C. Macgill, dean emeritus, University of Connecticut School of Law, for sharing stories, memories, and the photograph included here of his extraordinary grandaunt.

PICTURE CREDITS

For Kathy, Joyce, Rebecca, and
Elizabeth—and every girl who has a
passion and ideas of her own —JL

For my husband Frank, who
"electrifies" my life —SR

Calkins Creek
An imprint of Astra Books for Young Readers,
a division of Astra Publishing House
astrapublishinghouse.com
Printed in China

ISBN: 978-1-6626-8006-9 (hc)
ISBN: 978-1-6626-8007-6 (eBook)
Library of Congress Control Number: 2021925888

First edition
10 9 8 7 6 5 4 3 2 1

Design by Barbara Grzeslo
The text is set in Neutraface text Book.
The illustrations are done in watercolor with
digital drawing.